O, Say Can You See?

America's Symbols, Landmarks, and Inspiring Words

SHEILA KEENAN ★ illustrated by **ANN BOYAJIAN**

SCHOLASTIC INC.
New York   Toronto   London   Auckland   Sydney
Mexico City   New Delhi   Hong Kong   Buenos Aires

For Tom & James Cliggott, Nolan & Justin Finnerty, Kaitlynn Rose, Patrick
& Emma Keenan, and Brendan Duggan, with love from your liberal aunt.
Special thanks to my wonderful editor, Kate Waters; to assistant editor
extraordinaire, Elysa Jacobs; and to a terrific art director, Nancy Sabato.
—S. K.

To my grandparents, Franklin and Abigail Crocker, fine New England
Yankees, and Puzant and Siroog Boyajian, brave and resourceful
immigrants who came to this country and built a new life in America.
—A. B.

This book was originally published in hardcover by Scholastic Nonfiction in 2004.

ISBN-13: 978-0-439-59360-1
ISBN-10: 0-439-59360-3

12 11 10 9 8 7 6 5 4 3 2   7 8 9 10 11 12/0

Printed in the U.S.A.   66

This edition first printing, June 2007

The illustrations were created in pastel and colored pencil.

The display type was handlettered by Ann Boyajian.

The text type was set in Pike.

Book design by Nancy Sabato
★ ★ ★

CONTENTS

What is a symbol? 4

What is a SYMBOL?

There are stars and stripes T-shirts.

There are Statue of Liberty pencil sharpeners.

There's an eagle on our money

and Uncle Sam Halloween costumes.

Symbols are everywhere...
but where do they come from? What do they mean?
What *is* a symbol?

A symbol is something that stands for something else. Symbols can be important places, interesting objects, or inspiring words. The powerful symbols in this book stand for what the United States stands for: liberty, equality, and freedom.

There are more than 270,000,000 of us living in the United States. Some of our ancestors have been here for thousands of years. Some sailed here on the *Mayflower* more than 370 years ago. Some of us just flew here yesterday. We represent every race, country, and religion in the world. We speak different languages, eat different foods, and have different customs. But America's history and symbols belong to all of us. They're what make us feel proud, hopeful, and united!

The Pilgrims didn't actually land on Plymouth Rock in 1620.

Good thing! If they had, the 10-ton boulder would have ripped a hole in the *Mayflower*! The Pilgrims rowed to shore and settled nearby in what is now Plymouth, Massachusetts. But what about that rock?

In 1741, the colonists planned to build a wharf, or dock. It would cover Plymouth Rock. An old, old man said his father knew the Pilgrims and that this rock was their first landing place. People liked this story about early America (even though it wasn't true). So, they built the wharf around the rock.

During the American Revolution, colonists wanted a symbol of America's founding. Plymouth Rock was perfect! Over the years, the rock became more and more popular. And it started moving!

1774 Thirty teams of oxen and the strongest men in town pulled Plymouth Rock out of its sand bed under the wharf. The rock broke in half. Still, the top half looked pretty big. The oxen and men carted it away. They put it under an elm tree in the town square. The bottom half stayed under the wharf and was forgotten.

1834 Visitors to Plymouth Rock (the one under the elm) kept chipping off pieces for souvenirs. So, the rock was carted off to a new site in front of Plymouth's Pilgrim Hall. Along the way, the cart broke—and so did the rock! The two pieces were cemented back together and surrounded by an iron fence.

1867 People remembered the bottom part of Plymouth Rock. They ripped out the wharf and built a tall stone canopy over the rock. They had to cut a little bit off the rock so it fit underneath. (More souvenirs!)

1880 Plymouth Rock was united! The top part was moved and cemented to the bottom part. The year "1620" was carved into the rock.

1920 A symbol this important had to have a bigger monument! Plymouth Rock was hauled out and it broke again! A big new canopy with 16 columns was built and Plymouth Rock was lowered under it. It was back near where it originally was . . . and where it still is today.

If the walls could talk at INDEPENDENCE HALL,
they'd sound like an American history book! That's because our nation was born there.

In 1775, the United States didn't exist. The country was still 13 colonies that belonged to Great Britain. The colonists wanted more freedom. The British king refused to give it to them.

The Second Continental Congress voted to separate from Great Britain and signed the Declaration of Independence at Independence Hall, Philadelphia, in 1776. They approved designs for a flag and a great seal in 1777. They wrote the Constitution there in 1787.

Independence Hall was originally called the Pennsylvania State House. The Liberty Bell once hung in its tall bell tower. Philadelphia was our nation's capital for 10 years.

When in the Course of human events, it becomes necessary for one people to dissolve the politic bonds which h...

But by 1800, Congress, the Supreme Court, and the rest of our government had moved to the new capital in Washington, D.C. Independence Hall was empty. But not for long!

In 1802, Charles Willson Peale moved his museum of art and objects to Independence Hall. Peale was a popular American artist. He painted many famous pictures of American heroes, including 60 of George Washington. Peale also liked to collect things. He had 700 stuffed birds, 100 stuffed animals, a lamp with 200 candles, and mastodon bones!

The City of Philadelphia now owns and has restored Independence Hall. It looks as it did when its halls echoed with a bold call for INDEPENDENCE.

Would you like to live in a big WHITE HOUSE

with 132 rooms, 28 fireplaces, 35 bathrooms, 3 elevators, a tennis court, a swimming pool, a movie theater, and an 18-acre yard? If so, run for president.

The White House is the home and office of the president of the United States and his family. This grand building at 1600 Pennsylvania Avenue in Washington, D.C., is the most famous address in the United States. Every American president except George Washington has lived there. So have first ladies, first children, and first pets, from parrots to puppies to ponies.

In 1791, our first president, George Washington, chose the site for a President's House. It was a hill overlooking the Potomac River. The next year, James Hoban, an Irish architect, won a contest to design the building. Hoban drew a classic, three-story mansion. It would be made out of wood and brick and covered by sandstone. Construction began in 1792.

Our second president, John Adams, and his family moved into the President's House in 1800. The house was cold. The roof leaked, and the plaster walls were damp. The yard was full of construction rubbish. The President's House was not very presidential!

During the War of 1812, the British army burned down the White House. (But first, they ate the lovely dinner First Lady Dolley Madison had set out before she had to escape!)

The President's House was ruined. Its insides were burned out. The roof was gone. Only the walls stood and even they had cracked. But the house was still an important symbol to Americans, so James Hoban rebuilt it in 1815. The sandstone was sealed with whitewash, or paint, to protect it. The President's House was soon nicknamed the White House. It takes 570 gallons of paint to keep it white!

President Theodore Roosevelt made the White House name official in 1902. By this time, the mansion felt crowded. Roosevelt had the West Wing added.

The West Wing now houses the president's Oval Office, the Cabinet Room, and offices for the president's staff. Another Roosevelt, President Franklin Delano Roosevelt, had the East Wing added in 1942. It now has a theater and offices for the first lady and her staff.

President Harry S Truman arrived at the White House in 1945. Every president before him had left his mark on the building. Walls, ceilings, and beams had been drilled through to add plumbing pipes, gas lines, and electric and telephone wires. Rooms had been painted, redecorated, and sometimes moved. All of this began to weaken the wood-and-stone structure of the old house. Then a piano leg sank through a creaky old floor.

President Truman had most of the White House stripped bare to the outer stone walls. It was rebuilt with steel and concrete. This is the White House that stands today—with its original, 200-year-old outside walls!

The White House has six floors of rooms. The president holds meetings, gives televised speeches, and signs bills in the Oval Office. He sits at a carved oak desk made in 1880 from an old British ship.

The East Room is the largest room in the White House. It's used for ceremonies and concerts. A famous painting of George Washington hangs here. It is the only object that has always been in the White House. There's also a grand piano with carved

The Oval Office

golden American eagles on its legs. The East Room is lit by three chandeliers that each weigh 1,200 pounds!

The East Room

Expecting 140 people for dinner? They will all fit in the State Dining Room.

The Green, Red, and Blue rooms are used by the president or first lady to entertain official guests. The walls of the Green Room are covered in green silk cloth.

One look at the vivid color of its walls and you'll see where the Red Room gets its name. The furniture and decorations of this room are based on French designs.

The Blue Room is oval-shaped. It has sapphire-blue satin drapes and fancy wooden furniture painted gold.

The Blue Room

The first family lives in private rooms on the second floor of the White House.

The State Dining Room

No matter where you are
in much of Washington, D. C.,
you can look up and see a magnificent sight:
the soaring dome of the
CAPITOL BUILDING.

The Capitol Building is where Congress meets. The original plans for the Capitol were drawn by William Thornton, a doctor and amateur architect. It was designed like an ancient Roman temple with a dome in the middle and a wing on each side. The building was finished in 1811. Three years later, it all went up in smoke. The British army set fire to the Capitol during the War of 1812. After the war, everyone agreed: The patriotic thing to do was rebuild.

The Capitol then went through several design changes. The country was growing, which meant more people were in Congress.

In the 1850s, the Capitol's wings were made bigger so the Senate and the House of Representatives had enough room to meet. The Capitol is now 751 feet long and 350 feet wide. It has about 540 rooms and covers 16 ½ acres. But it's the part of the building that went *up* that is so famous!

When the Capitol Building got bigger, the original dome looked smaller. In 1856, the old wood-and-copper dome was replaced.

The new Capitol dome was designed by Thomas U. Walter. It is made of cast iron and weighs almost 9,000,000 pounds! It has classic columns and 108 windows. At the top of the dome is the bronze Statue of Freedom. She stands 19 feet, 6 inches high and weighs 15,000 pounds. The gleaming Capitol dome is 288 feet high.

Inside the Capitol is the magnificent Rotunda. This round room is 96 feet from side to side. It rises 180 feet high to the beautiful ceiling. At the very top, or "eye," of the dome, is an enormous round painting. It shows George Washington in the clouds with figures that represent liberty, victory, history, and science. Important scenes from American history are painted or carved along the walls of the Rotunda.

The Capitol Building has many, many works of art. There are 97 sculptures in the collection of the National Statuary Hall. They were sent by individual states and represent famous people from those states.

Four of the most important words of our democracy are carved in the front of the SUPREME COURT BUILDING:

EQUAL JUSTICE UNDER LAW

This means that our laws have to be just and fair. They have to apply to everybody in the same way. The United States Supreme Court, the highest court in the land, makes sure this motto is upheld.

The Supreme Court was created by our Constitution. The Court's nine judges, called justices, hear legal cases and decide whether government laws or rulings by other courts follow the Constitution.

When Washington, D.C., became our capital in 1800, the Supreme Court moved there. At first, the justices had to meet in the Capitol because they didn't have their own building.

In 1935, the Court finally got its own home. The judges didn't have far to move.

The Supreme Court Building is right behind the Capitol Building.

The Supreme Court Building looks like a 92-foot-high marble Roman temple. The marble came from Alabama, Georgia, Vermont, Italy, Spain, and Africa. It took 1,000 freight train cars just to carry the stone needed for the outside of the building.

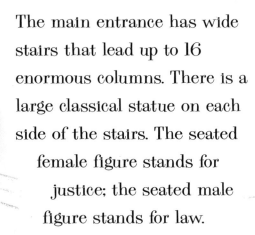

The main entrance has wide stairs that lead up to 16 enormous columns. There is a large classical statue on each side of the stairs. The seated female figure stands for justice; the seated male figure stands for law.

Above the building's entrance is a long sculpture of eight men and one woman dressed in ancient robes or armor. The middle figures stand for liberty, authority, and order. The others were modeled after real people, including three justices and the building's architect, Cass Gilbert.

The Court's 6 ½-ton bronze doors slide open. The Great Hall leads to the Court Chamber. Its ceiling soars up 44 feet. The Court Chamber has 24 white marble columns and a raised mahogany-wood bench where the justices sit. High above their heads are carvings of 18 famous lawmakers from world history. At the bench, our Supreme Court justices make history with each of the 80 to 100 cases they rule on every year.

the WASHINGTON MONUMENT.

It's the tallest building in Washington, D.C.

George Washington was elected our first president in 1789, winning every vote! Washington was our nation's first big hero—and people thought he deserved a big monument.

Construction on the Washington Monument began in Washington, D.C., on July 4, 1848. The monument was designed by architect Robert Mills. His original plan included a 110-foot-high Greek temple with an enormous sculpture of George Washington in a chariot on its roof. In front of the temple, there would be a 600-foot-tall obelisk.

The private project soon ran into trouble because of money and politics. Then the Civil War raged for four years. By 1876, the Washington Monument was just a half-built tower surrounded by scaffolds and swamps. The government took over.

You could climb 896 stairs to get to the top of

The reflecting pool, an the Washington Monumen

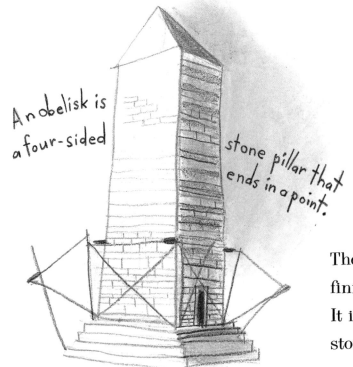

An obelisk is a four-sided stone pillar that ends in a point.

Congress voted for money to start building again. The plan became simpler: no temple, just the obelisk—but the world's tallest obelisk!

The Washington Monument was finished on December 6, 1884. It is still one of the world's largest stone structures.

The Washington Monument is 555 feet, 5 ⅛ inches tall. It took 36,491 bricks covered in marble to build it that high! The monument's walls support themselves; there is no framework inside. That's why the building is wider at the bottom, with thicker walls (15 feet), and narrower at the top, with thinner walls (18 inches).

Today, visitors cannot walk up the Monument. An elevator whisks you up to an observation platform in the pyramid top in 70 seconds. But you can climb down the 896 stairs. There are 193 stones embedded in the staircase walls. They were created in honor of George Washington. The stones come from all 50 states, some foreign countries, and some special groups. Some are made of unusual materials—Alaska's is jade and Arizona's is petrified wood.

Nevada's stone is made of granite.

elegant 2,000-foot-long rectangle of water, runs between and the Lincoln Memorial on the National Mall.

The real Abraham Lincoln was six feet, four inches tall. But the **Lincoln Memorial** statue of our famous 16th president is 19 feet high... *seated!*

(the real one)→

Abraham Lincoln was elected president in 1860 and served during the Civil War. That war nearly broke our nation in two. Northern and Southern states fought over slavery. President Lincoln fought to keep the United States just that—united. His ideas, words, and actions helped save and heal the nation.

The memorial to this beloved president is in Washington, D.C. It was designed by architect Henry Bacon and built between 1914 and 1922.

The Lincoln Memorial looks like an ancient Greek temple. The building is a marble rectangle, 188 feet long and 118 feet wide.

It is surrounded by 36 tall marble columns. The columns stand for the number of states at the time of Lincoln's death in 1865.

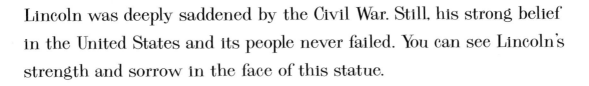

Inside the Lincoln Memorial is a 19-foot, 175-ton statue of the president sitting in a chair. It was designed by sculptor Daniel Chester French and carved from 28 blocks of white marble.

Lincoln was deeply saddened by the Civil War. Still, his strong belief in the United States and its people never failed. You can see Lincoln's strength and sorrow in the face of this statue.

The south inside wall of the memorial has Lincoln's Gettysburg Address carved on it. The president made this famous speech at the site of a terrible Civil War battle. He praised those who had died so that "government of the people, by the people, and for the people shall not perish from the earth."

On the north inside wall is Lincoln's second inaugural speech. The Civil War was almost over and Lincoln had been reelected president. In this speech, he asked all Americans, Northern and Southern, to feel "charity for all" and to "bind up the nation's wounds."

The STATUE of LIBERTY

is the world's most famous symbol of

FREEDOM,
OPPORTUNITY,
and HOPE.

She has stood tall over New York City's harbor for more than 100 years. When she was young, she was a warm copper brown. Steamships chugged past her, bringing millions of immigrants to America, their new home. Now she's a pale green. The boats still come, but they are ferries bringing millions of visitors to her feet.

The Statue of Liberty is an immigrant herself! She was made in France. The French people gave her to the United States to celebrate democracy. Frédéric-Auguste Bartholdi, a French sculptor, designed the statue he called "Liberty Enlightening the World" in 1870.

Some people say the statue is modeled after his mother's face and his wife's body.

The Statue of Liberty proudly holds a torch with a golden flame in her right hand. In her left hand, Liberty holds a tablet with July 4, 1776, the date of the Declaration of Independence, carved on it in Roman numerals. She wears a crown with seven spikes in honor of the seven seas and the seven continents. There's a broken chain under her feet, which stands for America's independence.

Bartholdi's Liberty is enormous . . . and hollow! The sculptor used a special method to create a copper "skin" that gives the statue its shape. More than 300 sheets of copper were hammered over the statue model. These metal sheets were only ³/₃₂ inch thick, about as

wide as a rubber band! They gave the Statue of Liberty its shape. But what was going to hold up its 62,000 pounds of copper skin? A "skeleton," of course!

Bartholdi contacted Alexandre-Gustave Eiffel, a brilliant French engineer. (He would later build the famous Eiffel Tower in Paris.) Eiffel designed an iron skeleton of four tall iron beams with cross braces. Attached to that is a network of metal bars, thinner beams, and brackets, which connect to the statue's copper sections. This system keeps the statue's skin from collapsing under its own weight. It also keeps the statue flexible, in case the weather gets too hot, too cold, or too windy. (When it's really windy, the statue sways three inches!)

162 stairs up

162 stairs down

Eiffel's ironwork skeleton was built in Paris. It rose 984 feet high. There was a double spiral staircase in the middle: 162 stairs up, 162 stairs down. (That's still how you get up to Liberty's crown—step by step!)

By 1884, the astonishing statue was finished. The Statue of Liberty loomed over Paris. At a ceremony on July 4, 1884, Bartholdi and the French government officially gave the statue to the United States. Now, it had to get there.

The Statue of Liberty was carefully taken apart. Every copper piece and iron bar was labeled. The 350 pieces were packed in 214 crates and shipped to New York City.

The ship docked in June 1885, but the crates stayed packed. There was nowhere to put the statue yet!

The French expected the Americans to build a pedestal, or base, for the Statue of Liberty. But not enough Americans had given money to build this base. Joseph Pulitzer, an immigrant who had become a successful publisher, was outraged. Pulitzer wrote about the problem in his newspaper, *The World.* He also printed the name of anyone who gave money— even a penny—for the pedestal.

pedestal pennies

Nickels, dimes, and dollars poured in. Even children gave. In five months, 121,000 people sent in $102,006.39. The pedestal builders went to work. By April 1886, they were finished. Then it took several more months to rebuild the statue on her pedestal.

Finally, on October 28, 1886, the Statue of Liberty was unveiled. Bartholdi pulled off the French flag covering her face. Cannons roared. Ship whistles tooted. Crowds cheered.

Lady Liberty was home at last!

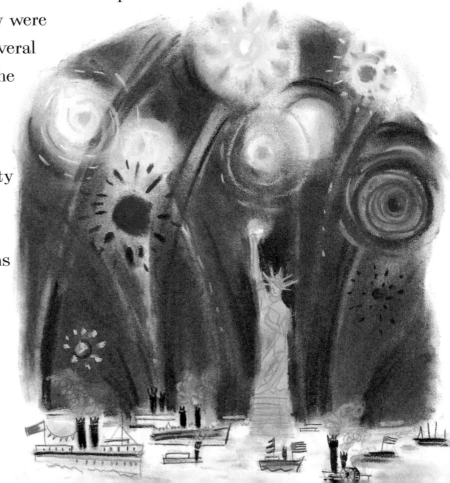

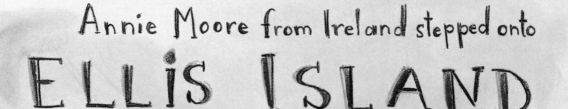

Annie Moore from Ireland stepped onto ELLiS ISLAND

on New Year's Day, 1892. She was given a $10 gold coin. Annie was the first of 12,000,000 immigrants who passed through this gateway to America.

Ellis Island is a small island in New York City's harbor. From 1892 to 1924, it was our country's busiest immigration center. Millions of people landed here. They brought clothes, dishes, bedding, bibles, teapots, tools, teddy bears, pots, pillows, even pickles with them.

Many did not speak English. They were tired and confused. The steerage passengers had been crammed in smelly, dirty, airless sections at the bottom of ships with several thousand other people. But they had made it to America. Now they just had to make it through Ellis Island.

Ellis Island opened in 1892. Its main building was big and fancy with four tall towers. Arriving immigrants climbed the steep stairs to the Great Hall Registry Room. They wore numbered tags that listed their names,

their home countries, and the ships they had sailed on. Ellis Island doctors checked them for signs of 60 different diseases in two or three minutes . . . or less!

People who passed the medical exams were then asked about their plans, if they had a job waiting, and how much money they had. All these tests usually took three to five hours. Most immigrants passed.

From the 1920s on, fewer people came through Ellis Island. New laws had cut down the number of immigrants. In 1954, the immigration center closed. The empty buildings started to fall apart.

More than 100 million people living in the United States today can trace their families back to relatives who came through Ellis Island. Many of them wanted to restore the main building. People all over the country donated things that someone in their family brought through Ellis Island. These 5,000 objects are now in the Ellis Island Immigration Museum.

MOUNT RUSHMORE
is the largest work of art in the world!

The presidents from left to right: George Washington, Thomas Jefferson, Theodore Roosevelt, and Abraham Lincoln

The giant sculpture of four American presidents was drilled, blasted, and carved into the solid granite face of a mountain ridge in the Black Hills of South Dakota. Each head is 60 feet high. And their creation is as amazing as the sculpture itself!

In the 1920s, a South Dakota state historian and a senator thought a large outdoor sculpture would bring tourists to their state. They got in touch with artist Gutzon Borglum.

Some people thought the whole monument idea was unnatural or silly. The Lakota Sioux were angry because the Black Hills are sacred to them. Not everyone agreed on what figures to carve or who would pay for the sculpture. Borglum was a difficult but determined artist.

28

Gutzon
Borglum

He fought to get his way. Work on Mount Rushmore began in 1927 and ended 14 years later. Congress paid most of the cost.

Borglum made large models of the heads. Then he used an ancient Greek measuring method called "pointing." The models were measured with a small pointing tool. The mountain was measured with an enormous pointing tool.

An inch on the model became a foot in the same place on the mountain.

Borglum's sculpture is high up Mount Rushmore. The workers had to climb 506 stairs, about 40 stories, just to get to work every morning! Work meant hanging in a harness off the side of the mountain while drilling with a jackhammer that weighed 75 pounds!

Half a million tons of rock were blasted away. Honeycombing brought out the details on the presidents' faces. Carvers drilled shallow holes close together, like a bee's honeycomb. Then they chipped off the rock in between these holes and bumped out any rough places with a special hammer.

And that's how...

George Washington got a 20-foot nose,
Thomas Jefferson an 18-foot mouth,
Theodore Roosevelt a 20-foot moustache,
and Abraham Lincoln 11-foot eyes!

Stars and stripes forever? Not quite.

Because our

FLAG hasn't always looked like this.

Our flag has only looked this way since July 4, 1960, when the 50th star was added because Hawaii had become a state. Like our country, our flag has a history.

American soldiers carried all kinds of flags during the Revolutionary War. One of the most famous was the bright yellow Gadsden flag. The rattlesnake on it was ready to strike . . . for freedom!

On June 14, 1777, the Continental Congress voted for a new national flag. It had 13 stripes and a constellation of 13 white stars in a blue rectangle.

DONT TREAD ON ME

But Congress didn't say how the stars should be arranged, or how many points they should have, or even which way to order the colored stripes.

The new American flag became known as the Stars and Stripes. Nobody knows for sure who designed it. There is no proof that George Washington asked Betsy Ross of Philadelphia to sew the first one.

After the American Revolution, more and more states joined the nation. By 1795, the flag had 15 stars and stripes. By 1818, there were 20 states. The flag was getting too big. Something had to be done!

the flag was getting too big!

On April 4, 1818, Congress voted to go back to using 13 stripes. They would represent the original colonies. Then, every Fourth of July, a star would be added for any new state added that year.

In 1912, a presidential order said that all American flags should be made the same way. The stars should have five points. They should be arranged in horizontal rows. Since we now have 50 states, these rows are staggered. There are five rows with six stars each and four rows with five stars each.

The Stars and Stripes has flown proudly—on buildings, battle sites, mountaintops, even the moon!

In 1942, Congress adopted the Flag Code. This code gives all the rules about how to handle a flag. It tells how it should be flown and how it should be folded. A folded United States flag looks like a triangle. This stands for the tricorner hats worn during the Revolution. If it weren't for the brave colonists under those hats, we wouldn't have a United States . . . or our famous flag!

1814 *Fort McHenry, Baltimore, Maryland* A giant 15-star, 15-stripe flag inspires Francis Scott Key to write our national anthem.

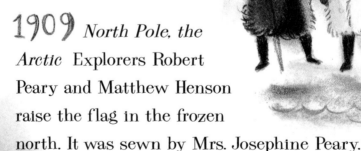

1909 *North Pole, the Arctic* Explorers Robert Peary and Matthew Henson raise the flag in the frozen north. It was sewn by Mrs. Josephine Peary.

1945 *Iwo Jima, Japan* Marines use a pipe for a pole and fly the flag after an important World War II battle.

1963 *Mount Everest, Tibet/Nepal* Barry Bishop climbs the world's highest mountain and plants our flag on top.

1969 *Moon* Astronaut Neil Armstrong becomes the first person on the moon. There is no air on the moon. The flag Armstrong plants has wires to hold it out, otherwise it would not wave.

2001 *World Trade Center, New York City* Rescue workers find a flag at Ground Zero. They raise it as a sign of hope and strength.

2002 *Earth, Space* A torn flag that once flew at the World Trade Center travels 5,000,000 miles aboard the space shuttle *Endeavour.* It also was displayed at the Olympics in Salt Lake City, Utah.

The LIBERTY BELL

is now silent,

but its message still rings loud and clear:

"PROCLAIM LIBERTY THROUGHOUT ALL THE LAND..."

The original metal bell weighed a ton! It was cast, or made, in London in 1752. The government of Pennsylvania had ordered it to be put on top of their State House (now Independence Hall). When the bell arrived, it was tested in the State House square.

The bell cracked the minute its clapper struck! Two metalworkers, John Stow and John Pass, offered to fix it. They smashed the bell, melted it down, mixed in new metals, and recast it.

Ding-dong-CRACK!!

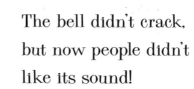

Ding-dong-THUNK!!

The bell didn't crack, but now people didn't like its sound!

Stow and Pass recast the bell again.
The third bell's E-flat note wasn't exactly
what everyone wanted, but it was good enough.

The State House Bell, as it was called, was used for
official business or important events. It rang on July 8, 1776, to
celebrate the first public reading of the Declaration of Independence.

In the 1830s, people who wanted the country's slaves freed started
calling it the "Liberty Bell" because of the words on it. Philadelphia's
Liberty Bell soon became a symbol of freedom to the whole country.

The Liberty Bell kept tolling. Finally, it cracked. No one is sure
exactly when. In 1846, it was repaired and rung in honor of George
Washington's birthday. It cracked—and never tolled again.

From 1885 to 1915, the Liberty Bell traveled around the country
seven times. It was mounted on a big, flat railroad car decorated
with flags, flowers, and banners. The train car was kept open so
everyone could see the Liberty Bell as it rolled down the tracks. It
was displayed at eight different World's Fairs and in 400 cities. People
couldn't hear the Liberty Bell anymore, but they could see it . . .
sometimes even kiss it! By the time it came home to Philadelphia
forever in 1915, the bell was America's most famous symbol of liberty!

Who is
UNCLE SAM?

A cartoon character from the 1800s?

A man in red, white, and blue on stilts in a parade?

A meatpacker from New York?

All of the above!

People all over the world recognize pictures of UNCLE SAM.

He's tall, thin, and has a small goatee, or beard, on his chin. He wears red, white, and blue. There are stars and stripes on his top hat, tailcoat, or pants. He is a human symbol of the United States.

In 1961, Congress passed a special resolution that said the Uncle Sam symbol was inspired by Sam Wilson of Troy, New York.

Sam Wilson fought in the American Revolution. Then he went to work as a meatpacker in Troy in 1789. His nickname was "Uncle Sam."

During the War of 1812, Wilson's company sold meat in barrels to the army. The barrels were stamped "U.S." This probably meant they were supplies for the U.S. government. But soldiers and government workers liked to say they were coming from "Uncle Sam" Wilson. Soon all supplies for the government were called "Uncle Sam's." Then the government itself was nicknamed "Uncle Sam"!

In the 1830s, newspaper artists started drawing cartoons of Uncle Sam. By the 1860s, they had given him the face and patriotic clothes that are now his trademark. The most famous picture of Uncle Sam was painted by James Montgomery Flagg in 1916–1917. It shows a stern Uncle Sam staring and pointing his finger right at you. The words below him say, "I WANT YOU!" The picture appeared on posters to urge people to join the U.S. Army during World War I and World War II.

Which would you pick for a NATIONAL BIRD?

The BALD EAGLE: a broad, seven-foot wingspan, a big head and beak, likes to soar high up in the air,

OR

the WILD TURKEY: a heavy body, a small head on a thin neck, likes to gobble and stroll in flocks on the ground?

I n the 1780s, Congress argued about this question for years. Benjamin Franklin, a famous politician, scientist, and Founding Father, wanted the wild turkey. He called it a "respectable bird" and a "bird of courage." He said the bald eagle was "too lazy to fish for himself" and stole other birds' food.

Franklin's idea didn't fly.

The Great Seal of the United States

On June 20, 1782, Congress agreed on a design for a Great Seal of the United States. The bald eagle was on it.

The eagle is powerful, fierce, and can live for up to 30 years. Strength and long life—Congress liked that in a national bird. Eagles perch high up in trees or on cliffs. They look independent and noble. Congress liked that, too.

Eagles have been used as symbols of power since ancient times. Congress did not like that. They wanted a new symbol for the new nation. So they made sure to pick the bald eagle, which is found only in North America.

You've probably seen this majestic bird on money, stamps, or holiday decorations. But you probably have not seen one in the air. North American bald eagles almost became extinct because of too much hunting and pollution! Laws now protect our national bird and its nests.

The bald eagle is not really bald. It has a white-feathered head. Its name comes from "piebald," which means having patches of white or black.

Everything on the GREAT SEAL of the UNITED STATES stands for something. It's a symbol with plenty of symbols!

Congress was very busy on July 4, 1776! First, they created the United States with the Declaration of Independence. Then they decided this great new nation better have a great seal.

A great seal is what countries use to stamp important official documents or treaties. Congress wanted a seal that showed what the United States stood for. Of course, everybody had different ideas about how to draw that! What about a Bible scene? Or a goddess of liberty? How about Hercules?

Congress debated these ideas and looked at sketches for six years. On June 20, 1782, they finally agreed on the design that's still used today.

There are a lot of thirteens on the Great Seal—stars, stripes, arrows. They represent the 13 original colonies: Connecticut, Delaware, Georgia, Maryland, Massachusetts, New Hampshire, New Jersey, New York, North Carolina, Pennsylvania, Rhode Island, South Carolina, and Virginia.

The Great Seal is kept in a glass exhibit case at the Department of State Building in Washington, D.C.—except for the several thousand times a year it's in use! You can see the Great Seal yourself any time. Just check out the back of a $1 bill.

The front, or obverse, of the Great Seal of the United States

A constellation of 13 five-pointed stars shows the United States is important among the free nations of the world.

Our national bird holds an olive branch with 13 olives and 13 leaves in one claw as a symbol of peace. The eagle holds 13 arrows in its other claw as a sign of war. The powers of war and peace belong to Congress.

The scroll says, "E PLURIBUS UNUM." This is Latin for "out of many, one" because we are one nation made up of many states.

The shield has 13 red-and-white stripes for the original states, under a blue bar that stands for the president and Congress.

The back, or reverse, of the Great Seal of the United States

The eye in the shining triangle is a symbol of divine providence, or the protection of one's god.

NOVUS ORDO SECLORUM is Latin for "a new order of the ages." This celebrates the birth of democracy in the United States in 1776.

ANNUIT COEPTIS is Latin for "He favors our undertakings." This phrase says that divine providence plays a role in the success of the United States.

The unfinished pyramid has 13 levels. The pyramid is a symbol of strength. The Roman numerals in its bottom level mean 1776, the year of the Declaration of Independence.

The DECLARATION of INDEPENDENCE

is the most important document in our nation's history.

When in the Course of human events,

John Hancock

In fact, it was the first to say that the United States of America _was_ a nation!

Thomas Jefferson had rented rooms in a house in Philadelphia in June 1776. They were across from a horse stable, which meant plenty of pesky horseflies! Day after day, Jefferson bent over the portable writing desk he had invented himself. He wrote feverishly with his quill, sometimes standing up! When the mornings were too hot, he soaked his feet in a tub of cold water. When night grew dark, he lit candles. After about two weeks, he was finished. The world was never the same.

In 1775, the 13 colonies in America still belonged to Great Britain. Many colonists were tired of being governed, taxed, and bullied by the British. They fought back. The Revolutionary War broke out. A year later, Jefferson and his fellow members of the Second Continental Congress made a bold choice: They voted for independence. Now they just had to tell Great Britain.

Congress wanted a statement explaining why the colonies should be free. Jefferson was well-read and a good writer. He was asked to write a draft for Congress. Words did not fail him! Jefferson organized the ideas and arguments of the Declaration of Independence into three

parts. The first part tells what rights people deserve and how they should be governed. The second part lists the unfair or wrong things Great Britain's king did to the colonies. The third part declares the colonies free, independent states. Nothing like it had ever been written before.

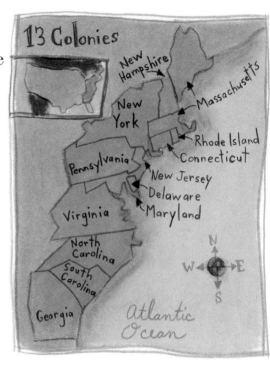

The Declaration of Independence is a powerful statement about freedom, liberty, and equality. It says right up front that "all men are created equal." Most of the world at the time was ruled by kings or queens. Equality was a daring idea. (Too daring even for the new nation! It took years and years for people other than white men to be equal under the law in the United States.)

The colonists also had new ideas about what it meant to be a citizen. That's why the Declaration says that people have the right to "Life, Liberty, and the pursuit of Happiness." This is what our democracy is all about. People choose for themselves how they will live and how they will be governed. If they're unhappy with the government, they have the right to change it. The colonists went to war to win this right. Now, we vote in elections to keep it.

Congress debated the Declaration of Independence for three days. They made 86 changes to Jefferson's draft, including one very serious change. They cut out Jefferson's attack on the slave trade. Slavery existed in Northern and Southern colonies. Some delegates would not support the Declaration unless the antislavery passage was removed.

On July 4, 1776, Congress voted to approve the Declaration of Independence. John Hancock, the president of the Continental Congress, signed it. He wrote his name really big. He wanted the British king to see it without his glasses!

The Declaration was then copied onto a piece of parchment, which the other members of Congress present signed on August 2, 1776. Signing meant you were a traitor to the king—and you could be hanged!

During the Revolutionary War, Congress had to keep one step ahead of the British army. They rolled up the Declaration of Independence and took it with them. After the war, it was stored in several different houses in Philadelphia.

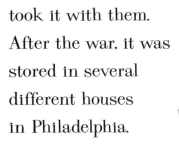

Then, in 1800, it was sent by boat to Washington, D.C., the nation's new capital.

The British attacked and burned Washington during the War of 1812. There was barely time to wrap the Declaration in a linen sack and cart it off to a safe house in Virginia.

During World War II, the Declaration was secretly packed into a metal box sealed with lead. It traveled by truck and train to Louisville, Kentucky. There, a whole cavalry troop escorted it to Fort Knox, where the government stores its gold.

The ideas of the Declaration of Independence will never fade—but its ink did! So, in the 1820s, a copy was made. The printing process got the Declaration wet. The ink faded some more.

Then the Declaration hung for 35 years in a government office in Washington, D.C. Sunlight beat down on it through a window. The parchment dried out and cracked. The ink kept fading. The Declaration, now nearly 100 years old, was disappearing!

Modern science saved the day! In 1952, protected by tanks, marines, and motorcycle squads, the Declaration of Independence was moved to its new home in the National Archives Building in Washington, D.C.

In 2003, the National Archives opened the Charters of Freedom exhibit. The Declaration, the Constitution, and the Bill of Rights are all displayed

in bulletproof metal cases. The cases are filled with a special gas and have special glass to protect the documents from pollution and sunlight. A computerized camera spots changes on the documents that are invisible to the human eye! At night, the cases slide into vaults in the wall.

Right after the Declaration of Independence was approved, John Hancock asked a Philadelphia printer to make several hundred copies for Congress. As far as we know, there are only 25 of these copies left. One of them was a very lucky find! In 1989, a man bought a picture for $4 at a Pennsylvania flea market. He only wanted the frame. When he took out the torn picture, he found one of the copies of the Declaration hidden behind it. He sold the Declaration for 2.42 million dollars. In 2000, it was resold for 8.14 million dollars!

The United States | CONSTITUTION and the BILL of RIGHTS show the world we are a democracy.

On May 25, 1787, 55 delegates from 12 of the 13 first states met in Philadelphia's State House (Independence Hall). They had a big job ahead of them: to figure out how the new United States should be governed. There were lots of big ideas!

The meeting lasted four hot, sweaty, buggy months. The delegates argued a lot. They voted over and over again, sometimes about the same point. They sweated when the windows were closed to keep their conversations secret. They swatted mosquitoes when the windows were open. When they were finished, they had written our Constitution. Now we could truly be the United States.

A constitution is the written ideas and rules that show how a country will be run. Our Constitution is only five pages long, but it has worked for more than 225 years. It set up the three branches of government we still have today.

EXECUTIVE

LEGISLATIVE

JUDICIAL

The executive branch makes sure laws are put into action. It includes the president. The legislative branch makes those laws. It includes Congress. The judicial branch settles arguments about the laws. It includes all of our courts. None of these branches is more powerful than another. This keeps the government balanced.

The Constitution also includes strict rules for making amendments, or changes, to itself. And some people wanted changes made right away!

Many people worried that the Constitution did not spell out the rights of individual people clearly. Five states would not approve it unless a Bill of Rights was added.

The Bill of Rights is the first 10 amendments to the Constitution. The First Amendment is the most famous. It protects freedom of speech, freedom of the press, freedom of religion, and the freedom to protest peacefully.

The Constitution was approved by the states and became law in 1788. The Bill of Rights became law in 1791. Together, they offer us our most important democratic right— that WE the people of the UNITED STATES are in charge of our nation!

WE the people of the UNITED STATES, in order to form a more perfect Union...

On September 14, 1814, Francis Scott Key grabbed an envelop from his pocket and scribbled a poem.

It became our NATIONAL ANTHEM.

The bombs started falling on Fort McHenry at 7 o'clock in the morning on September 13, 1814. They didn't stop for 25 hours.

Fort McHenry in Baltimore, Maryland, was attacked by the British during the War of 1812. Sixteen British warships shot more than 1,500 heavy bombshells at the American fort. By dawn, the smoke and fog began to clear. In the harbor, a young American lawyer eagerly clasped a telescope. Who had won the battle? Whose flag still flew? A slight breeze unfurled the fort's flag. It was the Stars and Stripes! The Americans had held the fort!

The young lawyer was Francis Scott Key. He had come to Baltimore to ask the British to free an American they held prisoner. Key went aboard a British ship outside Baltimore to discuss this. The British made him stay on board—he had heard too much of their attack plans.

When Key saw our flag still flying, he wrote his poem. You'll recognize the first eight lines:

> O! say, can you see by the dawn's early light,
> What so proudly we hailed at the twilight's last gleaming.
> Whose broad stripes and bright stars through the perilous fight
> O'er the ramparts we watched were so gallantly streaming?
> And the rocket's red glare, the bombs bursting in air,
> Gave proof through the night that our flag was still there.
> O! say, does that star-spangled banner yet wave
> O'er the land of the free and the home of the brave?

Key's poem was printed in newspapers. It was published as sheet music to the tune of a popular British song. It also got a new name:

The Star-Spangled Banner

In 1931, Congress voted to make it our national anthem.

The Pledge of Allegiance

October 12, 1892, was a whole new kind of school day. Twelve million kids in public schools all across the country stood up. Twelve million right hands were placed over hearts. Twelve million young voices rang out.

The Pledge of Allegiance was written in 1892 by Francis Bellamy, a Baptist minister. Bellamy was part of a group of educators who were planning a Columbus Day celebration in the country's public schools. It was to honor the 400th anniversary of Christopher Columbus's arrival in America. Bellamy's pledge was first printed in a family magazine called *The Youth's Companion*. Copies were also given to schools.

Our Pledge of Allegiance has changed since Reverend Bellamy first wrote it.

KABOOM! ★ ☆
Fireworks flash and explode in the night.

MMMM! A big, fat, tasty turkey
is ready for carving.

HURRAY!
Flags, floats, ★ ☆
and big bands pass by
in a parade. ★ ★

Everybody loves a HOLIDAY!

Holidays are really about remembering. We celebrate the brave people who fought in wars and those who fought for peace and justice. We honor the forefathers and foremothers who started our country and the workers who built it. We remember just how many things we have to be thankful for!

MARTIN LUTHER KING, JR. DAY

Third Monday ★ First celebrated: 1984

Dr. Martin Luther King, Jr. (1929–1968), was our most famous civil rights leader. In the 1960s, he led the fight for equal laws and voting rights for black people. Dr. King organized peaceful protest marches. His words and actions helped change laws—and people's lives! Dr. King was a powerful speaker. His famous speech, "I Have A Dream," is often read aloud on this holiday.

FEBRUARY

PRESIDENTS' DAY

Third Monday ★ First celebrated:
1782 (Washington); 1866 (Lincoln)

President George Washington (1732–1799), the "Father of His Country," helped found the nation. President Abraham Lincoln (1809–1865) kept it from falling apart during the Civil War (1861–1865). This holiday honors them and all the other men who have held the toughest job in the country: president.

MAY

MEMORIAL DAY

Last Monday ★
First celebrated: 1866
When the Civil War was over, people in Waterloo, New York, closed their shops, flew their flags only halfway up, and put flowers on the graves of soldiers to honor the people who had died. They started a tradition, and the idea spread. Today, we honor Americans who died in all wars on Memorial Day.

JUNE
FLAG DAY

June 14 ★ First celebrated: 1877

American flags fly on most holidays, but especially on June 14. On that day in 1777, the Continental Congress voted to create an American flag. One hundred years later, the United States Congress ordered flags flown on all government buildings on that date. Nearly 75 years after that, President Harry S Truman officially made June 14 flag day.

JULY
INDEPENDENCE DAY

July 4 ★ First celebrated: 1777

Happy birthday, America! This is our country's biggest holiday. It celebrates the Declaration of Independence. It was first celebrated on July 4, 1777, even before the country was independent, or free, from British rule! Bells rang. Cannons boomed. Bonfires blazed and fireworks sparkled in the night sky. People cheered wildly in the streets. And the birthday party continues every year!

SEPTEMBER
LABOR DAY

First Monday ★ First celebrated: 1882

You can't build bridges, buildings, towns, and cities without workers. Labor Day celebrates Americans who labor, or work. In the 1800s workers got together in groups and formed unions to get better pay, better hours, and safer workplaces. In 1882, some unions in New York City planned a picnic and parade. More than 10,000 people showed up for this first Labor Day celebration!

OCTOBER
COLUMBUS DAY

Second Monday ★ First celebrated: 1792

Christopher Columbus (1451?–1506) was a bold Italian explorer. He sailed to America in 1492 and thought he had discovered a "New World." It was only new to Europeans like Columbus. Millions of Native Americans had lived here for thousands of years. Columbus's arrival changed their way of life forever.

NOVEMBER
VETERANS DAY

November 11 ★ First celebrated: 1919

World War I (1914–1918) was the biggest war the world had ever known at the time. When it was over, President Woodrow Wilson declared a holiday. It was a day to celebrate peace at last. In 1954, President Dwight D. Eisenhower changed this holiday to Veterans Day to honor all Americans who have served in our military.

NOVEMBER
THANKSGIVING

Fourth Thursday ★ First celebrated: 1621

The Pilgrims celebrated the first Thanksgiving in 1621, but Thanksgiving did not become a big American holiday until 1863. For nearly 40 years, Sara Josepha Hale, a journalist, wrote about why we should celebrate this holiday. President Abraham Lincoln agreed with her. He declared a national day of thanksgiving. Finally, in 1941, Congress made Thanksgiving the fourth Thursday in November.

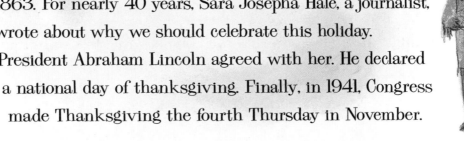

GLOSSARY

Words that appear in *italics*
are also defined in this glossary.

amendments changes made to *laws*

anthem a *patriotic* song

citizen a person who can legally live in a particular country and enjoy all the rights of that country

civil rights the freedoms and protections that legally belong to a *citizen*

Civil War (1861–1865) the war between the Union (the Northern states) and the Confederacy (the Southern states); also called the War Between the States

colonies areas where people settle that are ruled by the *governments* of other countries

constitution the written ideas and rules that explain how a country will be run

Continental Congress the *legislative* assemblies that governed the *colonies* and then the United States before the U.S. Constitution was adopted

democracy a system of *government* in which people elect their leaders

executive branch the branch of *government* that makes sure *laws* are put into action; it includes the president

Founding Fathers the leaders of the *Revolutionary War* and of the United States, which was created because of that war

government the people or organizations that run a country

immigrant a person who leaves one country to live in another

independent free; self-governed

judicial branch the branch of *government* that settles arguments about the *laws*; it includes all of our courts

laws the rules made by the *government*

legislative branch the branch of *government* that makes the *laws*; it includes our Congress

monument a building or statue that honors a person, event, or important idea

nation a large group of people who live in the same country under the same *government*

official approved by an authority

parchment an animal skin specially treated so that you can write on it

patriotic having feelings of loyalty to and love for your country

Pilgrims members of an English religious group who sailed to America and founded Plymouth Colony

republic a country or *government* that is run by leaders elected by *citizens*

Revolutionary War (1775–1783) the war fought by the 13 American *colonies* to gain their independence from Great Britain; also called the American Revolution

slavery a system that allows one person to own another; slaves were legally considered property, not people, in some parts of the United States before the *Civil War*

symbol something that stands for something else

veterans people who have served in a country's armed forces

War of 1812 (1812–1814) a war the United States fought and won against Great Britain because the British were interfering with American shipping, among other things

BOOKS TO READ

Bunting, Eve. *Dreaming of America: An Ellis Island Story*. Troll, 1999.

Catrow, David. *We the Kids: The Preamble to the Constitution of the United States*. Dial Books for Young Readers, 2002.

Curlee, Lynn. *Liberty*. Atheneum Books for Young Readers, 2000.

_____. *Rushmore*. Scholastic Press, 1999.

Dalgliesh, Alice. *The Fourth of July Story*. Aladdin Paperbacks, 1995.

Fink, Sam. *The Declaration of Independence*. Scholastic, 2002.

Fritz, Jean. *Shh! We're Writing the Constitution*. Paper Star, 1998.

Gibbons, Gail. *Soaring With the Wind: The Bald Eagle*. William Morrow & Co., 1998.

Grace, Catherine O'Neill. *The White House: An Illustrated History*. Scholastic, 2003.

Kay, Verla. *Tattered Sails*. Putnam, 2001.

Lawlor, Veronica (illus.). *I Was Dreaming to Come to America: Memories From the Ellis Island Oral History Project*. Scott Foresman, 1997.

Moore, Kay. *If You Lived at the Time of the American Revolution*. Scholastic, 1998.

Ryan, Pam Muñoz. *The Flag We Love*. Charlesbridge, 2000.

Sampson, Michael & Martin, Bill, Jr. *I Pledge Allegiance*. Candlewick, 2002.

Slate, Joseph. *The Great Big Wagon That Rang: How the Liberty Bell Was Saved*. Marshall Cavendish, 2002.

Spier, Peter. *The Star-Spangled Banner*. Yearling, 1992.

Waters, Kate. *Giving Thanks: The 1621 Harvest Feast*. Scholastic, 2001.

_____. *On the Mayflower: Voyage of the Ship's Apprentice and a Passenger Girl*. Scholastic, 1999.

_____. *The Story of the White House*. Scholastic, 1992.

Weitzman, Jacqueline Preiss & Glasser, Robin Preiss. *You Can't Take a Balloon into the National Gallery*. Dial Books For Young Readers, 2000.

AUTHOR'S NOTE

I used to live along the historic Freedom Trail in Boston, Massachusetts. My favorite pizza parlor was a few doors away from Paul Revere's house. American symbols were everywhere; after a while I took them for granted.

Years later, I ended up with a few hours to kill in Philadelphia, Pennsylvania. I'd never seen the Liberty Bell or Independence Hall, so I waited on a long, hot line to get into the Hall (though I probably wasn't as hot as the Continental Congress had been when they sealed themselves up in there more than 200 years ago!). The tour entered the Assembly Room. I looked at the wooden desks, the candles and the quill pens, the carved chair that George Washington once sat in. I was standing in the very room where the United States was born.

I was awestruck.

That's when I decided to write this book, to tell the story of why our national symbols are so powerful, to explain where they come from, and to show how ideas about them have changed over time.

Let true freedom ring.

—Sheila Keenan

ILLUSTRATOR'S NOTE

As I did the research for the illustrations for this book, I found out about some of the unusual, brave, and creative people who have shaped this country. It's pretty amazing to think about how the Declaration of Independence and the Constitution were written—that just a handful of thoughtful, brilliant, and very dedicated people put their heads together (and sometimes butted heads) to create the foundation of our nation. My favorite historical people are Thomas Jefferson and Dolley Madison. I admire Jefferson because of his amazing mind, and Dolley because she was such a clever hostess, leaving behind dinner for the invading British army so that she would have time to escape while they ate! And I became quite emotional when I drew the face of the statue of Abraham Lincoln. I think the sculptor really captured the expression of this sad, thoughtful man.

I made the illustrations for this book in pastel and colored pencil. Pastels are fun to work with because the colors are deep and intense, and because you can smear the colors around to blend them. But pastels are so powdery they can be hard to control when you draw small things. I draw on top of a pastel picture with colored pencils to add details.

—Ann Boyajian

INDEX

A Modern Symbol: Remembering 9/11/01

Most of the symbols in this book became famous, then familiar, over time. But symbols don't always come from the past. Sometimes they're created in the present.

On September 11, 2001, New York's World Trade Center was destroyed by terrorists. Several thousand people died in this attack. The twin towers became a symbol of America's pain and strength.

The World Trade Center had two soaring glass and steel towers. One stood 1,368 feet high, the other reached 1,362 feet. The 110-story towers sparkled in the sun or disappeared in the clouds. On a clear day, you could see for miles from the observation deck.

Remembering the World Trade Center in its glory and respecting the memories of the people who died there is important. It lets us turn an act of hate into a symbol of hope.

· · ·

This page is dedicated to people everywhere who are working to create a peaceful, free world.